Written by J A Aitchison

Cover design and Illustrations by: Chiara Scavuzzo

CW01426068

CONTENTS

SUPERHEART

THE SECRET
SUPERHERO

THE SUPERPOWER
OF KINDNESS

J A Aitchison

INTRODUCTION

If you met her in the street, Missy Matthews would look like a normal 10-year-old schoolgirl.

But she has a FANTASTIC secret – she is a SECRET SUPERHERO in Training!

What is even MORE fantastic, is that all her Secret Superhero Training happens in her dreams when she sleeps or sometimes when she daydreams.

When she closes her eyes and slips into the magical world between awake and sleep, she is visited by SUPERHEART, her Secret Superhero friend and mentor, who teaches her how to awaken her magical SECRET SUPERHEART POWERS that are sleeping inside her, and shows her how to use them to help others AHEAD of time...

Whenever Missy wakes up from her dreams SuperHeart's words always stay in her heart and mind, whispering to her...

"Now Missy, whoever you meet today, you just need to remember what we rehearsed..."

CHAPTER 1: ANOTHER SECRET MISSION!

As her alarm clock went off LOUDLY, Missy awoke up from another FANTASTIC superhero adventure dream, jumped out of bed, hugged Frank, her beloved dog and best friend, quickly pulled on her school clothes and ran downstairs for breakfast, doing her best to brush her wild, crazy hair as she ran.

"Mum! SuperHeart visited me again last night!" Her eyes sparkled and twinkled with excitement.

Missy's mum knew all about Missy's dream visits from SuperHeart and smiled wisely. *"How exciting! What did she prepare you for this time?"*

"Well, she told me I would meet lots of people today who need to be taught the Superpower of Kindness" said Missy. *"She reminded me how to connect with my heart, how to hear it speaking to me, so I will know exactly what to say and do at just the right time."*

"Wherever I am, I simply need to remember to close my eyes, breathe slowly, ask my heart to whisper the answers to me and repeat whatever it says." Missy demonstrated for her Mum, by closing her eyes, putting her hand over her heart and breathing slowly and deeply.

As the sun shone through the window, it caught the faint golden magical glow that sparkled and danced around Missy as she breathed through her heart.

"That's WONDERFUL!" said Mum, *"Eat up and let's get going, it sounds like you have a very busy*

CHAPTER 2: A GRUMPY START

Sure enough, as they started the walk to school, it wasn't long before Missy encountered her first opportunity to put SuperHeart's training into practice.

Mr Brown was an elderly neighbor who lived in Missy's street and who NEVER had a nice word to say about anyone or anything. Missy had often wondered WHY he was so grumpy with the world, but she had always been polite to him nevertheless.

Today he was the grumpiest she had EVER seen him. Before they had even walked past his house he had spotted them. *"Get your dog away from my garden!"* Mr Brown shouted crossly, angrily waving his walking stick in the air. Frank immediately put his ears down and quickly hid behind Missy's mum.

Missy stopped walking. She closed her eyes, placed her hand on her heart and started to breathe slowly. As she breathed she could hear the whispers of her heart speaking to her mind, and she repeated them quietly *"Feel the Superpower and magic of Kindness and may you always be kind."*

Immediately the sparkling golden glow formed like a shield around her. It couldn't always be seen clearly, unless the Sun (or Moon!) was shining at a certain angle to pick up the shimmer – but EVERYONE around her could feel it.

Mr Brown stopped shouting and eyed her curiously. He could feel it too…

Missy smiled at him and called back *"Don't you worry Mr Brown, Frank is a very well-trained dog, have a good day!"*

"Well done!" whispered Missy's mum with a wink, as they carried on walking.

CHAPTER 3: AN ANGRY ENCOUNTER

Before long, they encountered the second person in need of some SuperHeart magic that day. Missy, Mum and Frank stopped at the traffic lights, waiting patiently for the lights to change and tell them it was safe to cross the road.

As the lights changed, a driver who was driving much too quickly, was forced to brake hard and stop at the lights to let them pass. He was NOT a happy driver! As he screeched to a halt, he shook his fist at them and was clearly shouting at them inside his car, although thankfully they couldn't hear him.

Missy realized stopping in the middle of the

road would not be a good idea, so she quickly crossed the road before stopping in a safe place. The driver was still waiting for the red light to change, getting more angry and impatient by the second.

Missy closed her eyes, placed her hand on her heart, started to breathe slowly and listened...

"Feel the Superpower of Kindness..." she repeated... *"May you feel calm and always be kind"*... Once again, the sparkling golden shield started to grow and glow around her...

The driver stopped shouting and eyed Missy curiously...

At that moment, the lights turned green and he drove off slowly, looking slightly confused at what had just happened...

"Great job Missy!" whispered her Mum with a

knowing smile.

CHAPTER 4: AN INJURED DISCOVERY

Missy and her Mum were almost at the school gates when Missy suddenly stopped walking.

"Did you hear that Mum?" she asked, listening intently for the faint sound she had just heard.

There it was again! It was a very faint whimpering sound and it seemed to be coming from under a nearby hedge. Missy followed the sound to a large bush and peered underneath.

There she discovered a small, frightened-looking dog with an injured paw. The dog immediately started to growl at Missy.

Although she adored animals and was never afraid of them, she knew much better than to touch the injured dog which was likely in a great deal of pain. As her mum called the emergency vet, she kneeled down at a safe distance, closed her eyes, put her hand on heart and started to breathe slowly...

"Feel the Superpower and Magic of Kindness... may you feel no pain or be afraid" she whispered quietly to the injured animal.

The dog immediately stopped growling, put its head on one side and watched her with curious big brown eyes...

"Good girl Missy" said her Mum, *"You run into school now, Frank and I will wait here for the vet to arrive, she's already on her way."*

CHAPTER 5: A SAD FRIEND

As Missy arrived at school, she soon discovered the next person in need of her help that day. Tobo was a good friend of Missy's who was usually very pleased to see her, but today he could barely raise a smile.

"Tobo, what's wrong?" Missy asked immediately, sensing he was more sad than angry.

"Nothing, I'm fine." Tobo snapped grumpily and a little too quickly. *"I don't want to talk about it!"* he said, and he folded his arms defensively. *"There's nothing you can do about it anyway."*

Tobo was usually cheerful and optimistic, so Missy knew that whatever had happened must have been quite serious to make him behave this way. She sensed it was best not to ask any more questions, but she also knew better than Tobo that there definitely WAS something she could do about it...

Without saying another word to him, Missy closed her eyes, put her hand on her heart and started to breathe slowly... the sparkling golden glow immediately surrounded her and Tobo too.

"Feel the Superpower of Kindness... May you no longer feel sad and always be kind" she said silently to Tobo, as the words of her heart flowed to her mind.

Highly sensitive to the emotions and feeling of others, Missy instantly sensed Tobo's mood shift and lighten beside her, as she carried on sending him some extra kindness for a few moments more. She knew he could feel the magic and she also knew he would open up to her when the time was right.

"*Sorry,*" Tobo whispered, sounding far less irritable. "*It's not your fault, I'll tell you later...*"

CHAPTER 6: A NERVOUS START

Just then, their teacher Mrs MacDonald, swept into the classroom with her arms full of books and a new boy with dark curly hair doing his best to hide himself behind her.

"Hello everyone!" she said cheerfully, *"We have a new face to welcome into class today – this is Will"* and she gently guided Will to stand in front of the class.

Will looked very nervous and his cheeks were red with embarrassment. He looked down at the floor, doing his best not to catch anyone's eye.

At that moment, poor Will turned completely

white – and was promptly sick on the floor. As the class started either yelling at the smell or laughing at the ensuing chaos, poor Will fled from the room, and Mrs MacDonald quickly ran after him.

"Poor guy!" whispered Tobo to Missy. *"And I thought I was having a bad day!"*

Missy immediately went into action. Although Will had left the room, she could still picture him in her minds' eye. She closed her eyes, put her hand on her heart once again and started to breathe slowly...

"Feel the Superpower and Magic of Kindness... know you are welcomed and that you belong here" she whispered. As she did so, the magical golden glow grew around her, only this time it grew bigger and BIGGER until it filled the classroom and started to drift out of the door and down the corridor to the washroom,

where Missy knew Mrs MacDonald would be cleaning up poor Will.

CHAPTER 7: AN UNKIND MOMENT

Soon the headteacher appeared.

"Children, while we clean up the classroom, you can have a short time outside – I'll join you all in just a few minutes."

With a cheer, the children quickly headed out to the playground. As she ran outside with the others, Missy suddenly overheard Arn, who liked to describe himself as the school's Supreme Bully, laughing with his friends at poor Will's predicament.

"What a loser! But did you see the best bit - he was sick all over Sprout's shoes! Ha! Serves him right for being the class jerk!" Arn laughed

unkindly.

Sprout was his equally unkind nickname for Russell Archer, the quietest boy in the class, who they called Sprout simply because his name rhymed with Brussel...

Missy immediately stopped, closed her eyes, put her hand on her heart and started to breathe slowly...

"Feel the Superpower and Magic of Kindness... May you feel sympathy and always be kind" she whispered. Once more, the sparkling, magical glow grew around her...

Arn turned around quickly and looked at Missy suspiciously. *"What weirdness are you doing Little Missy Perfect?"* he asked slowly. He couldn't explain it, but he suddenly felt VERY uncomfortable and not at all like his usual bullying self.

Missy just smiled at him, which made Arn feel even MORE uncomfortable and he quickly ran off, his so-called friends following like sheep behind him.

CHAPTER 8: A WISE VISIT

Delighted with the unexpected time outside, Missy headed straight to her favourite place in the whole school, the big oak tree at the edge of the school field. She loved to sit or lie under it and listen to it whispering to her.

She lay down in the grass, smiling as she looked up through the branches, listening to the breeze as it rustled the leaves. She felt the familiar delightful tingling feeling all over her body as she started to drift into a magical daydream...

As soon as she slipped between the worlds, SuperHeart was waiting for her as always and gently landed on the grass beside her...

"You've done so well this morning Missy" SuperHeart said with a smile. *"You had some tough situations to handle, but you did so brilliantly and I'm VERY proud of you."*

"Always remember, there are NO situations where Kindness can't help. When people are grumpy, angry, frightened, sad or feel the need to bully others, often they already feel that way about THEMSELVES, for many different reasons. So, they say and do grumpy, angry, defensive things to PROTECT themselves or make themselves seem tougher than they truly feel. Being irritated or angry back to them will not help them and never solve that – and will usually make things MUCH worse... What they REALLY need is the magic and superpower of kindness just as much, if not more so, than the people they are being angry or unkind towards. It may sound silly and upside down, but I know you

understand."

Still laying on the grass with her eyes closed, Missy nodded.

"You see," SuperHeart explained, *"Mr Brown was in a LOT of pain with his arthritis today and was grumpy BEFORE you walked past. The driver was already running late so was actually cross with HIMSELF for getting up late, not with you for crossing the road. The little dog was in pain and frightened, and what you didn't know about poor Tobo, is that his little sister dropped her ENTIRE bowl of breakfast porridge on the school project he's been working on for weeks. As for Arn, well his older brother had been very mean and thumped him this morning, but HE got the blame for starting it! So he was simply taking his frustration and anger out on someone else."*

"Always remember," SuperHeart continued, "that everyone is dealing with their own silent

difficulties every day. But instead of giving them back more grumpiness, anger, frustration or unkindness, you gave kind thoughts, kind words, kind feelings and a smile...you made them remember they can CHOOSE a better way to feel. I think you will be quite surprised at the changes you made along the way today Missy...."

Just then, Missy stirred from her daydream as she heard the headteacher calling them all back into class.

With a swoosh of red cape and a flurry of golden sparkles, SuperHeart was gone, the leaves of the tree rustling in the breeze as she flew away.

CHAPTER 9: A

BRAVE APOLOGY

As Missy ran back across the playground, Arn ran up to her. He looked very apologetic and rather embarrassed.

"Umm, I don't know what that strange thing was you were doing back there, but I felt weird afterwards, like you had been kind to me even though I didn't deserve it. I know that sounds even more bizarre and I can't really explain it, but I just wanted to say sorry – and thanks. I... I...know what I said about that new kid was mean, and I know how I would have felt if it had been me." He hesitated. *"I know I've been unkind to Sprou...I mean Russell, too. Please don't say anything to Mrs MacDonald Missy, I really will*

try to be kinder and more sympathetic."

Arn looked down, scuffing the toes of his shoes on the ground. *"It's not an excuse, but I was SO mad this morning. My brother was thumping me and calling me names from the moment I got up."*

Missy grinned at him *"And you got the blame for starting it, right?*

Arn looked at Missy in amazement. *"Yeah, how did you know?!"* he asked.

"Oh, just a lucky guess," said Missy casually.

"Well you're totally right. When I pushed him back and called him an idiot my dad heard ME and I got the blame – so no football training tonight. It's just so unfair!" Then he sighed. *"But I guess I chose to push him back – I could have walked away. And none of that was Will or*

Russell's fault. I get it, Missy, I really do. Thanks for listening – and whatever that Thing was you did just now."

Smiling, they ran back into class to join the others.

CHAPTER 10: A KIND OFFER

As the children settled back into the classroom, Tobo slid into the spare seat beside Missy.

"I'm so sorry I was miserable and snappy earlier. My little sister managed to totally wreck my Egypt project this morning – you know how long it's taken me to build those pyramids. I was SO mad, but that was no reason to be rude and unkind to you Missy, I'm truly sorry. I felt especially bad for being short with you and I had this WEIRD feeling you were being kind to me, even though you didn't say anything and even though I definitely didn't deserve it."

Missy grinned at him. She was certain

she could hear SuperHeart gently laughing nearby, although she couldn't see her she could feel she was around and somewhere close...

"It's ok Tobo, really it is," said Missy kindly *"but I'm sure the porridge can be scraped off and the models can easily be repainted. The damage might not be as bad as you think!"*

Tobo looked at her curiously. *"How did you know it was porridge she dropped on it when I hadn't told you?"*

"Lucky guess" said Missy, shrugging her shoulders and with a twinkle in her eyes. *"Anyway, forget it, I can come over tomorrow after school to help you rebuild it if you like?"*

Tobo beamed at her. *"That would be amazing! Yes please!"*

Just then Mrs MacDonald swept into the class.

"Children, thank you all very much for behaving so responsibly earlier. I'm sure you will all be pleased to know Will felt much better by the time his mum came to collect him. He was actually surprisingly calm! He even said he thinks he's going to like it here! I know you will all do your very best to make him feel welcomed when he's back tomorrow."

Once again, Missy smiled happily to herself.

CHAPTER 11: A
HAPPY WAVE

After school, Missy ran to the school gates where her Mum and Frank were waiting for her. Frank and Missy missed each other very much during the day, and were inseparable at all other times. Missy hugged him tightly as he woofed with happiness to see her.

"How was your day?" asked Mum.

"Well," said Missy, *"SuperHeart sure was right, there were a LOT of people needing a LOT of kindness today!"* and as they started to walk home, Missy told her Mum all about the adventures at school that day...

Missy was still excitedly describing the

impact of Kindness on Arn, when they stopped at the traffic lights again.

Slowing down to stop at the lights and let them cross, was the SAME driver from the morning – only now he looked like a VERY different person. He looked happy!

First, he smiled and waved at them as they crossed, then he lowered the window and called to them.

"Hey, I wanted to apologise for how I behaved this morning" he said sheepishly. *"I was running late for an important meeting and was mad at myself. I behaved badly and I'm really sorry."* He paused.

"I felt very strange for the rest of the day, like you had been kind to me, even though I didn't deserve it. I couldn't stop thinking about it all day. It really made me think, so um... thanks."

Missy smiled at him. *"It's when people are angry and unkind that they need kindness the most"* she said wisely.

The driver looked at her in amazement. *"Young lady, I think that is the wisest thing anyone has ever said to me. You are so very right. I will do my best to remember your wise words, thank you."* He drove off, still smiling.

"Quite a transformation!" said Missy's mum with a wink.

CHAPTER 12: AN APOLOGETIC GIFT

As they neared home, Missy could feel and hear her stomach rumbling – being a Secret Superhero made her very hungry!

Just then they walked past Mr Brown's gate. His front door flew open and he stood there waving his walking stick at them. Frank instantly hid behind Missy's mum again.

Only this time, Mr Brown did not look angry at all – he was smiling at them and was waving his walking stick only to get their attention.

"Hey there Missy!" he called *"I have something for you – please come here for just a minute. Yes,*

your dog can come too."

As they walked up the garden path, Mr Brown stood at his front door beaming at them.

"Young lady, I owe you a VERY big apology for how grumpy and unkind I was to you this morning." He sighed. *"When you're an old man like me, whose legs don't work as well as they used to, I get very frustrated with myself at times. My arthritis is always more painful in the morning and today I took that out on you. It was unforgiveable and I'm truly sorry. So here, I made you this"* and he handed her a large, delicious-looking chocolate cake!

"You have always been so friendly and kind to me and your dog is probably the most well-behaved dog in the neighbourhood. I felt very strange for the rest of the day, like you had been kind to me, even though I didn't deserve it. It really made me think, so can you please forgive

this silly, grumpy old man?"

Missy handed the cake to her mum, dropped her bag on the step and hugged him. *"Mr Brown, there is nothing to forgive, it's when people are grumpy and angry that they need kind thoughts sent to them, not angry ones. That would only make them grumpier!"*

Mr Brown hugged Missy back. *"Young lady, in all my years, I think that is the wisest, kindest thing that anyone has ever said to me. You are indeed right Missy. I will do my very best to remember your wise words every day."*

As they waved goodbye Missy whispered to her Mum *"Another kinder heart in the World!"*

CHAPTER 13: SOME EXCITING NEWS!

Back at home, Missy had just started to enjoy a large slice of the chocolate cake when the phone rang.

Her mum answered it. It was the emergency vet Missy's mum had phoned that morning, when they found the injured dog.

"Oh, that's fantastic!" Missy heard her mum say. *"My daughter will be very happy to hear that, she was the one who found him. I will tell her the exciting news!"*

"What's happened Mum?" asked Missy curiously.

"Well, fortunately that injured dog you found this morning was wearing a tag so was easily reunited with it's very worried and relieved owner. A delivery driver had left the side gate open last night, so the dog escaped and they think it must have been hit by a car. If you hadn't heard the whimpering, it wouldn't have received the urgent care it needed and it might even have died! The owner is so happy to have their dog back, that they are giving you a £100 reward!"

"Wow! That's amazing, but I really don't think I did anything to deserve that!" said Missy in amazement.

"Well, to many people their pets are members of the family, which makes them priceless and irreplaceable – think how you would feel if something happened to Frank! This is just their way of thanking you. So, thanks to you being so kind to others today, you now have enough *money to buy that new bike you wanted!"* said her Mum.

Missy was so excited to hear this – she had been saving her pocket money and even her birthday money, so she could buy a new bike – and now she had enough!

"Hmmm, well SuperHeart did tell me that the Superpower of Kindness would magically come back to me in ways I least expect!" Missy said thoughtfully.

CHAPTER 14:

ANOTHER SUCCESSFUL

MISSION!

That night, Missy happily snuggled into bed after her busy superhero adventure, with Frank curled up in his basket, dreaming Superdog dreams. Missy's mum kissed her goodnight and hugged her tightly.

"You made a big impact on the world today Missy" said her Mum gently. *"You brought cheerful kindness to others and reminded them that there is always a better way to be. You reminded me too!"* she added with a wink.

Missy liked to leave her curtains open just a little every night, so she could see the Moon and the stars twinkling and sometimes even a Shooting Star.

Tonight, there was a Full Moon and the shining golden orb glowed like a giant lightbulb in the sky. Missy often wondered what lay beyond the atmosphere of Earth. Planets, stars, moons, galaxies, maybe even other life. Maybe that's where SuperHeart came from – she really didn't know.

But one thing Missy DID know in her heart, was that if she could be visited in her dreams by a Secret Superhero, then there was a LOT more magic and adventure in the Universe than most people believed...

Missy closed her eyes and smiled as she started to feel the wonderful tingle of approaching sleep. At that moment, as if she had heard her thoughts, SuperHeart landed gently beside her.

"I'm so proud of you, for all that you achieved today Missy" said SuperHeart. *"I hope you have also learned never to underestimate the magic and power of true heart-felt kindness. The combination of your genuine heart, together with your kind thoughts and words send out magical ripples – not just to the people in need who you met today, but to the people and families they went home to or met throughout their day too. Here, take a look..."*

SuperHeart gently placed a finger on Missy's forehead, between her eyebrows, and although her eyes were still closed, instantly Missy could see a movie running in her mind's eye. She saw Mr Brown laughing on the telephone to his daughter and grandson. She saw the driver arriving home with a big hug for his children, immediately playing football with them in the garden. She saw the dog happily being reunited with its owner and

Arn at home, laughing with his brother as they played a computer game together. She even saw Tobo kindly reading his sister a bedtime story.

"Now, there is just one more thing I would like you to do before you sleep Missy..." said SuperHeart....

CHAPTER 15: MOST IMPORTANTLY OF ALL...

"In fact," said SuperHeart, *"as the next step in your Superhero Training, I would like you to do it every night before you sleep and every morning as soon as you wake up."*

"What's that?" Missy asked sleepily, but still paying very close attention to SuperHeart's words.

"There's one more very important person who needs the magical kindness of your heart today."

"Frank? Mum? Dad?" asked Missy.

"Well yes," said SuperHeart, "but that's not who I mean."

"I mean YOU, Missy. Tune into your heart as I showed you and send kindness and magic to YOURSELF."

Still with her eyes closed, Missy placed her hand on her heart, slowed her breathing and said quietly "May I feel the Magic and SuperPower of Kindness and may I always be kind."

As she said the words, the sparkling golden glow around her grew bigger and brighter than ever and it lit up the whole room as though it was lit by brilliant sunshine!

"You must always remember to include yourself Missy – that way you send the magic, power and energy of loving kindness to every cell of your body, which helps to keep it healthy and strong, and it also makes you a shining example of everything that you are here to teach others."

"A very wise teacher once said "One kind heart is more powerful than a thousand unkind hearts. Being kind is not a weakness, it gives you the silent strength of thousands."

Missy smiled happily, still with her hand on her heart, "Thank you SuperHeart, for your wisdom and for showing me the magic and true Superpower of Kindness."

SuperHeart leaned over and kissed her gently on the forehead. "May you sleep in peace and magic, and wake in kindness and joy… I will see you again very soon Missy."

And with a swoosh of her red cape and a flurry of golden sparkles, SuperHeart was gone, but she would indeed be back very soon, to guide

Missy on her next Secret Superhero Mission…!

The End

SUPERHERO
TRAINING TIP!

*Imagine that we are much more
magical than we think...*

**Why not try SuperHeart's Secret to the
Superpower of Kindness Yourself?**

Step 1: Begin by thinking of someone
you know who needs the Magic and
Superpower of Kindness today.

Step 2: Put your hand on your
heart and close your eyes.

Step 3: Breathe in slowly, counting to
4, then breathe out slowly, counting
to 4. Do this a few times.

Step 4: Now imagine the Magic of Kindness is all around you. You breathe in kindness for yourself and breathe out kindness to everything around you!

Step 5: Now think of the person you chose who needs the Magic and Superpower of Kindness.

Step 6: Keeping your eyes closed and your hand on your heart, think of the person and say silently or out loud *"Feel the Magic and Superpower of Kindness... and may you always be kind."*

Step 7: Keep breathing slowly in and out as you think of this person. You can even imagine them inside a sparkling bubble of golden light!

Step 8: Keep breathing in and out the

Magic and Superpower of Kindness for as long as you like - not just for this person, but also for yourself and others.

Step 9: Pay attention to how you now feel, and to any wonderful, kind things that happen to you in the next few days…

And always remember, as SuperHeart says…

"For a few moments every night before you sleep and every morning when you wake up, send the Magic and Superpower of Kindness to YOURSELF, for everything you learn and succeed at every day, and for being UNIQUELY, MAGICALLY and BRILLIANTLY YOU!"

Just like Missy, you too, are now a Secret SuperHero in Training!

Look Out For More Adventures With Missy In

SUPERHEART
THE SECRET SUPERHERO'S

OTHER EXCITING MISSIONS!

Book 2: The Superpower Of Imagination

Book 3: The Superpower
Of Spoken Wishes

Book 4: The Superpower Of Gratitude

ABOUT THE AUTHOR

Jeanette Aitchison

At her happiest when creating magical, superpowered creations to inspire and empower others, Jeanette is an author, wellbeing consultant and hypnotherapist who lives in the land of magic and mystery (also known as Scotland) with her husband, three children and a ridiculous amount of Lego.

Contact Jeanette or sign up to learn more about the next SuperHeart mission:

https://www.quantumlifecoaching.co.uk

Printed in Great Britain
by Amazon